Teacher's Notes
Water and Rivers

Manda George

Series editor | Sue Palmer

Contents

OXFORD
UNIVERSITY PRESS

OXFORD
UNIVERSITY PRESS

Great Clarendon Street, Oxford OX2 6DP

Oxford University Press is a department of the University of Oxford.
It furthers the University's objective of excellence in research, scholarship,
and education by publishing worldwide in

Oxford New York

Auckland Bangkok Buenos Aires Cape Town Chennai
Dar es Salaam Delhi Hong Kong Istanbul Karachi Kolkata
Kuala Lumpur Madrid Melbourne Mexico City Mumbai Nairobi
São Paulo Shanghai Taipei Tokyo Toronto

Oxford is a registered trade mark of Oxford University Press
in the UK and in certain other countries

British Library Cataloguing in Publication Data

Data available

ISBN 0 19 834874 6

3 5 7 9 10 8 6 4

Typeset by Fakenham Photosetting, Fakenham, Norfolk

Printed in the UK

What is Oxford Connections?

Oxford Connections is a set of 12 cross-curricular books and related teaching materials for 7 to 11 year olds. The books will help you teach literacy through a science, geography or history-based topic. Each book provides the material to cover two units from the QCA Schemes of Work for the National Curriculum in England and Wales, and the non-fiction literacy objectives for one whole year of the National Literacy Strategy. (You can find a grid of where the QCA and NLS objectives are covered on p 48 of these notes and on the inside back cover of the pupils' books.) The books can be used to focus primarily on literacy or on science/geography/history.

Literacy

Pupils need different literacies. As well as traditional texts with different purposes and audiences, they also need to be able to understand and write material presented in different forms such as diagrams, bullet points, notes and Internet displays, particularly when working with non-fiction.

Oxford Connections supports the development of these different literacies. It focuses particluarly on reading and writing non-fiction, and will help children use effectively the different non-fiction text types (report, explanation, instructions, recount, discussion, persuasion).

Using these books will help pupils to focus on the two main elements which make a text type what it is:

◆ The language features used (for example, present tense for instructions, and past tense for recounts, use of commands in instructions, etc.).

◆ The structure of the text (for example, chronological order, in the case of instructions or recounts).

The structure of a text can be represented as a diagram or framework, showing visually how the parts of the text fit together, which are the main points and how they are developed, etc. (A very common example of this type of presentation is a timeline, which shows events which have happened in the past, as a continuum, the order of which cannot change.) In this book, we refer to material presented in this diagrammatic way as *visual (visual reports, visual explanations,* etc.).

Pupils will learn to read and to present information visually (by using frameworks), thus developing good note-taking skills, and consolidating their understanding of how texts are structured. The visual texts in particular are accessible to those pupils who need more support. Using frameworks to plan their own writing will also help improve all pupils' planning and drafting/editing skills.

In this book, we have used icons to represent the different sorts of frameworks you can use, called *skeletons*. These are referred to in the *National Literacy Strategy Support Materials for Text Level Objectives* (DfES 0532/2001). They can be used as an aide-memoire to help pupils remember the structure of each text type. They appear on pp 6–47 to show you what text types are on the pupil's book pages.

Recount		Explanation	
Instructions		Persuasion	
Non-chronological report		Discussion	

Using *Water and Rivers* to teach literacy

There are step-by-step instructions to teach pupils how to read and write the different text types, on pp 18–47 (a six-page section for each text type). They follow this model:

Each six-page section contains:

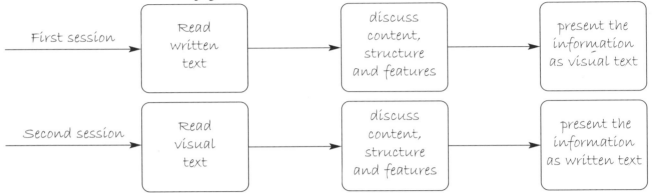

Two pages of step-by-step instructions taking you through the process described in the diagram above. They will help you analyse a written text, and then produce a visual version of that text with a group of pupils. You will then analyse a visual text, producing a written version.

A page describing the relevant text type.*

An example of the text type (an excerpt from *Water and Rivers*) for you to read and analyse with pupils.*

The same example with language features highlighted for your reference.*

A visual version of the written text for your reference.*

*can be photocopied as handouts, a poster or an OHT

There are page-by-page notes on how to use the material to cover other aspects of literacy on pp 6–17. These page-by-page notes also show how to use the material in the pupils' book for the particular subject covered, e.g. geography.

Speaking and listening, and drama

The discussion which is inherent in this method of learning should improve pupil's speaking and listening skills. As well as helping pupils to organize and structure their ideas before writing, visual texts should prompt pupils to use the relevant language features orally, as well as in writing. Additional speaking and listening, and drama activities such as those below, can be used to further reinforce the children's learning.

Retelling – events can be retold by an individual or by groups taking a section from a visual recount.

Role-play – using the visuals created by the whole class to ask/answer questions in role, being the person in the recount or taking one side of the argument etc.

Mini plays – retelling an event or following an explanation visual to show how something works. Pupils could be the different parts of whatever is being explained.

Puppet plays – retelling an event or following an explanation visual.

Freeze-frame – pupils in groups could show sections from a recount visual or report visual. They could show different aspects of a discussion.

TV/radio reports – demonstrating knowledge using a visual report as a TV/radio report. In a TV report images could be used either pictorially or by the use of freeze-framing.

TV demonstrations – follow an instruction visual or explanation visual to demonstrate making something or explaining how something works.

TV/radio interviews – retelling events in recounts or use report visuals while interviewing another pupil in role.

TV/radio adverts – using a persuasive visual to make adverts.

Illustrated talks – using the visual as a prompt.

Hot seat – answering questions in role – either as a persuasion, report or recount.

Debates – using discussion visuals to have debates between individuals or groups.

Using *Water and Rivers* to teach geography

Water and Rivers contains all the material you need to cover this topic, and to achieve the objectives of the *QCA Scheme of Work for the National Curriculum Geography* Units 11 and 14 (recommended for Year 5 pupils). There are page-by-page notes on how to use the material for geography on pp 6–17. You can find a grid showing where the QCA objectives are covered on p 48 of this book, and on the inside back cover of *Water and Rivers*.

Which year group should I use *Water and Rivers* with?

Water and Rivers has been written for Year 5 pupils (9–10 year olds). However, if your school places the topic in another year group, the geography material contained in *Water and Rivers* will still be suitable for use with other age groups. Although all of the non-fiction literacy objectives for Year 5 are covered, many of the objectives for other year groups are also supported. Most of the six non-fiction text types are covered in it, and language features for Years 3, 4 and 6 are highlighted in the relevant sections.

SCOTLAND AND NORTHERN IRELAND

NB throughout this introduction the term *Year 5* has been used to mean 9–10 year olds. The references in the grid on p 48 are to the *National Literacy Strategy* and to the *QCA Scheme of Work for the National Curriculum*. However, *Water and Rivers* is suitable for use with P6 in Scotland and in Northern Ireland, since it supports many elements of the *National Guidelines, 5–14* and *The Northern Ireland Curriculum*. The geography content of *Water and Rivers* does not conflict in any way with either *National Guidelines, 5–14* or *The Northern Ireland Curriculum*.

Geography

Use these pages as advance organizers to provide pupils with an overview of the work to be conducted:

concept map shows the main areas to be covered and the links between them.

contents page shows how this information has been organized in the book.

◆ Use the quotations as an aide for using the contents page – ask the pupils to find what is being mentioned.
◆ Return to the pages occasionally during teaching to help the pupils see how their learning and understanding is building up.
◆ Use as a revision aid, asking pupils to summarize what they know about each aspect.
◆ Use the concept map at the end of the topic to review all areas of the topic covered.

Literacy

Help pupils to recognize the similarities and differences between the concept map and contents page:

◆ that they contain the same information, differently organized;
◆ that the concept map provides an overview of the ideas contained in the book and how they are interlinked; the contents page provides a linear guide to the way these ideas are organized;
◆ that the contents page gives numbers for ease of reference.

Throughout your use of the pupils' book, demonstrate how to use the contents page – along with the index (see p 17 of these notes) – to access information when required.

Geography

◆ Link to science work on the water cycle (QCA Science Unit 5D).

Key concept
◆ To revisit the components and sequence of the water cycle.

Key vocabulary
◆ *evaporation, condensation, water cycle, river, lake, spring, pond, ocean, water vapour, hail, snow, droplets*

Suggested activities
◆ Use the picture to orally explain the water cycle.
◆ Remind pupils about evaporation.
◆ Make a 3D model of the water cycle – either a large model for a class display or the pupils make their own models.

Literacy

Page 4	Page 5
○→☼→◑	○→☼→◑
written explanation	visual explanation

◆ When reading the text, discuss how texts of this type need to be carefully organized in order to present a clear explanation to the reader. Discuss how diagrams, charts and illustrations help the reader to gain understanding.
◆ Make an explanation skeleton (a cycle flowchart) of the various stages in the water cycle – include any information from the text.
◆ Discuss how each stage of the cycle can be one part of the skeleton. These stages can then be a guide to paragraphing when they write up the notes.
◆ Prior to writing up the notes discuss the language features of explanation text (see pp 36–41 in these notes).

Geography

Key concept
◆ Develop skills in observation, questioning, collecting and recording evidence.

Key vocabulary
◆ *rain, cubic centimetre (cc), rain gauge, funnel*

Suggested activities
◆ Follow instructions to make rain gauges.
◆ Decide how long to collect and measure rainfall, e.g. one week, one month.
◆ Record results in a variety of ways, e.g. bar chart, pictogram or graph.
◆ Make a class display – example rain gauges, water cycle display, results.

Literacy

Page 6	Page 7
○►○►○►	○►○►○►
written instruction	written instruction

These pages are used as a featured example to teach the reading and writing of **instruction** text (see pp 24–29 of these teacher's notes).

Geography

Key concepts
◆ Availability of water is linked to climate and weather.
◆ Climate is affected by a number of different factors.

Key vocabulary
◆ *rainfall, river, lake, source, spring, ocean, dam, ice-cap, glacier, climate, drought, humidity, latitude, altitude, well, bore hole*

Suggested activities
◆ Research a desert climate or a tropical climate. Use report skeleton notes to choose criteria, e.g. temperature, rainfall.
◆ Locate chosen area on a map/atlas. Refer to the map on pp 8–9 of pupils' book to find out if it has a hot/wet climate.
◆ Present information as a chart or as a graph.

Literacy

Page 8	Page 9
written report	written report

◆ Identify the features of a report text (see pp 32 of these notes).
◆ Look at the organization of the text and discuss whether it is successful. Look at the layout, captions, pictures etc.
◆ Demonstrate how to make notes from the spread by making a report skeleton (see pp 30–35 of these notes) as an introduction to the research in the geography lesson. Include information from the pictures.

Geography

Key concepts
◆ To understand the importance of clean water and plentiful supply.
◆ To understand that too much water can be as devastating as too little water.
◆ Know about aid agencies' work on water provision in less economically developed countries.

Key vocabulary
◆ *drought, dust bowl, flood*

Suggested activities
◆ See notes for pp 8–9 on p 7 of these notes.

Literacy

Page 11	Page 11
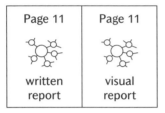	
written report	visual report

These pages are used as a featured example to teach the reading and writing of **report** text (see pp 30–35 of these teacher's notes).

Discuss how the text is presented as a newspaper report using features such as headlines, leaders, columns etc.

Geography

Key concepts
◆ That water is a universal need.
◆ That access to water varies in different parts of the world.

Key vocabulary
◆ *rain, water supply, water hole*

Suggested activities
◆ Compile a list of the various uses of water in Christina's village and make a report skeleton (see pp 30–35 of these notes).
◆ Compare water usage in Christina's village with the pupils' own water usage at home.
◆ Discuss what might help Christina and her family to have a better supply of water.
◆ Watch and discuss the WaterAid video.

Literacy

Page 12	Page 13
⊢+⊢+→	⊢+⊢+→
visual recount	visual recount

These pages are used as a featured example to teach the reading and writing of **recount** text (see pp 18–23 of these teacher's notes).

Geography

Key concepts
◆ That water is a universal need.
◆ That access to water varies in different parts of the world.

Key vocabulary
◆ *tap, sanitation, drought, contaminated, wells, pumps*

Suggested activities
◆ Use the web links in the bibliography to find out how to 'help thirsty people', how other aid agencies help – take notes and make a report skeleton.
◆ Find the countries or areas that have needed/will need help.
◆ Make a poster or leaflet about how people can help.

Literacy

Page 14	Page 15
*≶	*≶
*≶	*≶
*≶	*≶
written persuasion	written persuasion

◆ When reading the text explain to the pupils that persuasive writing aims to convince the reader about a point of view. Note the use of 'strong language' to persuade, and the use of evidence to back up main points (for features of a persuasion text see p 44 of these notes).
◆ Turn text into notes using a persuasion skeleton focussing on the different points in the three paragraphs – access to clean water, contaminated water and cheap water supply –as well as the text in boxes – effects of drought and aid agencies.
◆ Make persuasive leaflets about same or similar topic using the notes.

Geography

Key concepts
◆ Understand that access to water varies in different parts of the world.
◆ Learn about jobs in a settlement.
◆ Learn about the environmental impact of a local activity.

Key vocabulary
◆ *handpump, drainage, channel*

Suggested activities
See the notes for pp 14–15

Literacy

Page 16	Page 17
○►○►○►	○►○►○►
visual instruction	visual instruction

These pages are used as a featured example to teach the reading and writing of **instruction** text. (See pp 24–29 of these teacher's notes). Note how the numbers on each section of the flowchart help to signify the sequenced steps of the process.

Geography

Key concept

◆ That local activities may have knock-on effects for the environment.

Key vocabulary

◆ *pollution, irrigation, reservoir, source, hydroelectric dam, flooding, lake, sediment, ecosystems*

Suggested activities

◆ Explain that the page is about a real project although the text is fictional.
◆ Find out about the Three Gorges Dam (use bibliography) and whether it has been built.
◆ Investigate other dams and the effects on the local environment and people.

Literacy

Page 18	Page 19
*≶ *≶ *≶ visual persuasion	*≶ *≶ *≶ visual persuasion

These pages are used as a featured example to teach the reading and writing of **persuasion** text (see pp 42–47 of these teacher's notes).

When reading the text, draw pupils' attention to the fact that the main points presented in both sides of the argument are backed up with supporting evidence.

Hold a class debate to explore both sides of the argument presented.

Geography

Key concept

◆ That water is used for a variety of purposes.

Key vocabulary

◆ *source, irrigation, sewage, litre, hydroelectric*

Suggested activities

◆ Link to pp 12–13, 26–27 and 28–29 of pupils' book.
◆ Identify water usage at school.
◆ Make report skeletons about how water is used at home/school/other.
◆ Consider any recent droughts/hosepipe bans.
◆ Investigate why we should not waste water.

Literacy

Page 20	Page 21
visual report	visual report

◆ Use the example on homes as a starting point and remind pupils of the features of report texts (see p 32 of these notes). In groups, pupils write up the notes on the spread. Each group works on one section, e.g. transport, and finds additional information and pictures from other sources.
◆ Make a class display of the reports.
◆ Write letters to agencies to find out how they can save water at school.
◆ Make posters to put up reminding people how to save water.

Geography

Key concepts

- Water is transported in a variety of ways.
- Water supply can be controlled using a valve system.

Key vocabulary

- *stopcock, tap, drain, sewer valve, mains, meter, drainage*

Suggested activities

- Tour the school and use a map to indicate where water can be found.
- Interview the caretaker – ask questions – *Where does water come into the school from the mains? is there an outdoor stopcock? indoor stopcock? Cold water storage? Hot water cylinder? What happens to the sewage?*
- Use the cross section of the house on the page to help draw a rough cross section of the school. Highlight where water comes in and out of the building as well as where it is used.

Literacy

Page 22	Page 23
⊙→☼→⊙	⊙→☼→⊙
written explanation	written explanation

These pages are used as a featured example to teach the reading and writing of **explanation** text (see pp 36–41 of these teacher's notes).

Geography

Key concepts

- To know what happens to water once it has been used.
- To understand the importance of a clean water supply.

(Link to Science Units 4D and 5D)

Key vocabulary

- *reservoir, river, purification, sewage, drain, water cycle, fresh water, filter bed, chlorine, fluoride, aquifer*

Suggested activities

- Visit a sewage works.
- Discuss why water needs to be treated – use the pages to help answer the question.
- Collect water samples from school pond, playground etc.
- Test the water by observing and drawing/recording what they see and also by smelling it.
- See if they can improve the appearance and smell by either filtering and/or boiling the water.

Safety note: **Do not let the pupils taste the water.**

Literacy

Page 24	Page 25
⊙→☼→⊙	⊙→☼→⊙
visual explanation	visual explanation

- Discuss with the pupils the relative merits of written text and diagrams for conveying information of this kind.
- Make explanation skeleton notes from the pages (cycle flowchart).
- Remind pupils about the language features of explanation text (see p 38 of these notes).

Geography

Key concepts
◆ Water is necessary for a range of uses.
◆ Water wastage is an issue for everybody.
◆ Reducing water consumption could help to improve the environment.

Key vocabulary
◆ *hosepipe, tap, litre, ml, millilitres*

Suggested activities
◆ Ask pupils to keep a diary of their water usage at home over a week.
◆ Record their results as a graph (how much water is used at one time) and compare their results.
◆ Discuss water wastage/why they should not waste water.

Literacy

Page 26	Page 27
++++ ++►	++++ ++►
written recount	written recount

These pages are used as a featured example to teach the reading and writing of **recount** text in the form of a diary (see pp 18–23 of these teacher's notes).

Geography

Key concepts
◆ Clean water is essential to modern-day living.
◆ Water is polluted in a range of ways.
◆ Reducing water consumption may help to improve the environment.

Key vocabulary
◆ *pollution, drain, sewage, pollutants, groundwater*

Suggested activities
◆ Link to environmental issues.
◆ Investigate water pollution – make a report skeleton of all the possible causes of water pollution.
◆ Find out more about what the Environment Agency does (see pp 42–43 of the pupils' book).
◆ Contact Friends of the Earth for any additional information – use their website (see bibliography).

Literacy

Page 28	Page 29
*≶	*≶
*≶	*≶
*≶	*≶
written persuasion	written persuasion

◆ Following the reading of this text discuss other forms of persuasive writing pupils have encountered, e.g. advertisements, brochures, fliers etc.
◆ Use the page to make persuasion skeleton notes of the main points.
◆ Revisit the features of the persuasion text (see p 44 of these notes).
◆ Write a leaflet for a younger audience – discuss how the language used will need to be appropriate.

Pages 30–31

Geography

Key concepts
- The notion of 'owning' water is a complex concept.
- Water companies provide an essential service.

Key vocabulary
- *rain, purification, water butt, sewage, septic tank*

Suggested activities
- Look at and discuss a water bill.
- Find out who the local water company is (see bibliography).
- Find more about the water company for the area.

Literacy

Page 30	Page 31
*≶ *≶ *≶ written persuasion	*≶ *≶ *≶ written persuasion

These pages are used as a featured example to teach the reading and writing of **persuasion** text (see pp 42–47 of these teacher's notes).

- Discuss the differing points of view and that they are presented in the form of a letter of complaint and response.
- In considering the two letters, draw pupils' attention to the viewpoints from which they are written. Note the use of language to create tone and style.
- Write a letter to the local water company in order to find out what they do and how they work.

Pages 32–33

Geography

Key concepts
- The importance of a clean water supply is essential to modern-day living.
- Dirty water can cause serious disease.

Key vocabulary
- *river, tap, sewer, well, pump, sewage, cesspit, contaminated*

Suggested activities
- Link to literacy work on note taking. Highlight the purpose of research and the importance of establishing a 'brief' for the kinds of note to be made. This is because it is important that the notes they take are specifically related and not generalized.
- Find out more evidence about water problems in Victorian times using a KWL grid (K – what do we know? W – what do we want to find out? L – what have we learnt?).
- Find any significant evidence about local problems in Victorian times.

Literacy

Page 32	Page 33
visual report	visual report

- Use the notes from the page to make a report skeleton (structuring paragraphs etc.).
- As a drama activity, pupils recreate television reports about the state of the water supplies and sewage systems in Victorian times – use the skeleton as a starting point. Have a main reporter but also 'outside' reports where 'Victorian' characters are interviewed – use the skeleton to ask questions.
- Write up a report about problems in Victorian times (see pp 30–35 of these notes).

Geography

Key concepts
◆ That there are connections between farming, industry and climate.
◆ The cause and effects of changes in a river.

Key vocabulary
◆ *irrigate, river, source, delta, swampland, desert, dam, navigable*

Suggested activities
◆ Find where the River Nile is on a globe and then a map of Africa.
◆ Make skeleton notes about the key facts about the river.
◆ Using the Internet, CD-ROMs and other printed sources research other rivers and make 'top trump' cards of the key facts – *Where is it? How long? Any dams? How many countries does it flow through? How many towns does it flow through?* The cards could be designed and written as an ICT activity on a text programme.

Literacy

Page 34	Page 35
written report	written report

◆ When reading the text, discuss how information is organized in sections to help the reader.
◆ Identify the text features of a report text (see p 32 in these notes).
◆ Make report skeleton notes.

Geography

Key concept
◆ To understand that water can be transported in a variety of ways.

Key vocabulary
◆ *irrigation, river, shaduf*

Suggested activities
◆ Discuss what irrigation is – look at ancient and modern methods – use a range of books for research. Link to literacy work on note taking.
◆ Design and technology - there are opportunities to link work on irrigation with the workings of a water pump.
◆ Make a model of a shaduf.
◆ Link to any work on Ancient Egyptians.

Literacy

Page 36	Page 37
visual explanation	visual explanation

These pages are used as a featured example to teach the reading and writing of **explanation** text. See pp 36–41 of these teacher's notes.

Discuss with pupils how the diagrams are effective in presenting this type of information to the reader.

Use the pages to make instruction skeleton notes to help make a model of a shaduf.

Geography

Key concepts

◆ Rivers cause changes in the surrounding environment.

◆ That over time the landscape can alter dramatically due to the river flow and the associated processes.

Key vocabulary

◆ *river, source, mouth, valley, erosion, deposition, tributary, meander, waterfall, oxbow, silt*

Suggested activities

◆ Use the notes from the literacy session while visiting a river.

◆ Draw sketch maps of a river and label the main features.

◆ Look at erosion and deposition in more detail using other sources.

Safety note: **Pupils must take extra care when near water.**

Literacy

Page 38	Page 39
○-☼-☼	○-☼-☼
visual explanation	visual explanation

◆ Discuss with pupils how diagrams and illustrations are sometimes used in explanation text to help the reader.

◆ Remind pupils of the language features of explanation text (see p 38 in these notes).

◆ Make an explanation skeleton of what they might find on a river visit.

Geography

Key concepts

◆ To understand the way a river works.

◆ That different sections of the river cause the landscape to look different.

◆ To use geographical vocabulary to describe and explain sections of the river.

Key vocabulary

◆ *river, ordnance survey map, velocity, gradient, depth, deposit, silt, eroded*

Suggested activities

◆ Make a list of what the pupils did in the recount.

◆ Use the list as a guide for a practical activity.

◆ Visit a river.

Literacy

Page 40	Page 41
┼┼┼→	┼┼┼→
written recount	written recount

◆ Note how the text is written in the first person and the past tense. Also discuss the inclusion of detail to make the recount interesting for the reader.

◆ Write notes in the form of a report skeleton and/or research skeleton while doing their river research.

◆ Use the skeletons to write own recount of their river research.

Geography

Key concept
◆ That there are a number of factors which may cause changes in the river, e.g. pollution.

Key vocabulary
◆ *river, polluted, aquatic*

Suggested activities
◆ Follow the instruction skeleton during the visit to the river.
◆ Use the ticklist to identify whether the water is polluted or clean.

Safety note: **Pupils' must take extra care when near water.**

Literacy

Page 42	Page 43
O→O→O→	O→O→O→
written instruction	written instruction

◆ Discuss with pupils the key features of instruction text, e.g. imperative tense, chronological order, use of numbered bullet points etc. These features help the reader when following the instructions.
◆ Make an instruction skeleton from the instructions on p 42 of the pupils' book to support the river research.

Geography

Key concept
◆ To use vocabulary associated with Water and Rivers.

Suggested activities
◆ Use these pages to search for the meanings of key vocabulary to further pupils' understanding of different aspects of Water and Rivers. Identify words from reading that are unknown and use the glossary to further understanding and to clarify information learnt.

Literacy

Use these pages to demonstrate how to locate information confidently and efficiently through using a glossary.

◆ Remind pupils of the purpose of a glossary: to explain the meaning to the reader of any words or terminology that are specific to the subject of the text.
◆ Using some of the key words identified in both the pupils' book and in these teacher's notes, scan the glossary to find some of the meanings. Point out that the words are in alphabetical order rather than subject order.

Geography

Use the bibliography to find other sources.

Pupils could create own bibliography based on texts they have used to research particular geographical concepts.

Literacy

Use these pages to teach the pupils the purpose and function of a bibliography.

Point out to pupils that a bibliography:

◆ collates all the references to other sources made in the text;
◆ provides a reference point for further reading;
◆ avoids the author being challenged for using someone else's work (plagiarism);
◆ is organized alphabetically using the surname of the author;
◆ provides the ISBN number as well as the title of the reference;
◆ contains some of the following sources: books, websites, articles, periodicals or journals.

Use the bibliography to find further details about one area of water and rivers. Ensure the pupils use a wide range of sources referenced.

Discuss how different source material, e.g. websites, books etc. is organized, e.g. thematically, alphabetically etc. Compare details provided in *Water and Rivers* with material found in a different source.

Geography

Key concept

◆ To develop an understanding of different aspects of water and rivers.

Suggested activities

◆ Ask pupils to brainstorm areas they know about water and rivers and record, e.g. on a whiteboard. Using the index as a reference, identify key areas that go together, e.g. plumbing, mains water, sewage and fit into the areas defined on their whiteboards. Show how they link to the conceptual map on p 2 of the pupil book and the contents page.

Literacy

Use these pages to locate information confidently and efficiently through using an index.

Remind pupils of the purpose of an index: to enable readers to find, at speed, specific information. Use the index to find specific information. Point out the following:

◆ At times, it is quicker to use an index sometimes than using the contents.
◆ Skimming is a more general approach than scanning.
◆ An index sometimes doesn't take you to the information you want – you may have to go to a number of pages.
◆ Both skills can be used to obtain information quickly but have different purposes, e.g. scanning when you want to know something specific, and skimming if you want a general overview before obtaining details or making a close read.

Teaching pupils how to read and write recount text

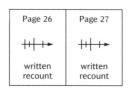

Page 26	Page 27
written recount	written recount

Reading a recount text

Read pp 26–27 of *Water and Rivers* pupils' book with the pupils. You will need:

◆ the written recount on pp 26–27 (the text-only version on p 21 of these notes can be enlarged/ photocopied/ made into an OHT for annotation)
◆ p 20 of these notes enlarged/photocopied/made into OHTs for annotation

SHARED READING ACTIVITY

Audience and purpose
Talk about how the intended audience and purpose affects language and layout.

Audience – personal journal is usually for the writer (in this instance it is for the class).

Purpose – to find out about daily water usage.

SHARED WRITING ACTIVITY

Content and organization
Show pupils how the content of this recount is organized by demonstrating its content in a recount skeleton (see p 23 of these notes). Events are organized in chronological order and divided into sections which will make suitable paragraphs. Highlight that in this journal recount there is no introduction of background information because it is a personal journal, e.g. Toby does not need to know who and where he is.

SHARED READING ACTIVITY

Language features and style
Return to the text and talk about the way language has been used to create the effects the author intended (see annotated version p 22 of these notes). Note useful features for later use in pupils' own writing, e.g. connectives signalling time (*afterwards, when, next, first then*); how detail is added to interest the reader (*… because it would have been too difficult to measure how much water we used*).

INDEPENDENT ACTIVITY

Independent activity
Pupils could use their own water diaries to create recount skeleton notes based on the skeleton notes from Toby's diary. As an alternative, pupils could write skeleton notes of how they have used water in school.

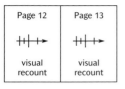

Page 12	Page 13
visual recount	visual recount

SHARED
READING
ACTIVITY

PAIRED
READING AND
WRITING
ACTIVITY

SHARED
WRITING
ACTIVITY

INDEPENDENT
WRITING
ACTIVITY

Writing a recount text

Use pp 12–13 of *Water and Rivers* pupils' book as a basis for pupils' own recount texts. You will need:

◆ the visual recount on pp 12–13

◆ p 20 of these notes enlarged/photocopied/made into OHTs for annotation

Content and organization

Revise the content and organization of the recount text from the previous session (see p 23 of these notes).

Pairs of pupils discuss the visual recount on pp 12–13 of the pupils' book and identify key events to create a recount skeleton.

Language features and style

Remind pupils of the language features and style of recount texts (see p 20 of this book).

Audience and purpose

Discuss the audience for pupils' recounts (other class members) and the purpose (to retell events).

Demonstrate by writing a short introductory paragraph to set the scene, highlighting key language and organizational features. Explain that they are writing in the third person, not the first – like Toby's diary, which is a personal recount. Their writing will be a formal and impersonal recount.

This is a day in the life of Christina, a native of Ghana in Africa. It is very hot where she lives and there is very little rain. There is no water supply in the village and Christina has to walk to the water hole to get water for her family.

Ask the pupils in pairs to orally compose the next sentence, e.g.

At 7am Christina sets off from her home to begin the long journey to the water hole.

Return to paired talk to consider how additional information could be included, in order to interest the reader, e.g. *Where is she walking?* Ask pupils in pairs to compose next two sentences using an appropriate connective device to link the information, e.g.

About an hour later she finally arrives. There are many other people collecting water, as this is the only supply of water for miles around.

Pupils complete the recount independently.

⊬⊬⊬→ About recount text

Audience and purpose

Audience – someone who may not know much about the events

Purpose – to retell events that actually happened

Sometimes you may know more about the age or interests of your reader

Content and organization

- **introductory paragraph** sets the scene, so the reader has all the basic facts needed to understand the recount

Answer the questions who? what? when? where?

- **introduction** often also hints at the main event of the recount
- events written in **chronological order** – time order

First this happened ... then this happened ... next ...

- **closing statement** – sentence(s) or paragraph to bring the recount to an end

Use your introductory sentence to help you write your conclusion. If the introduction is a question then answer it in your conclusions

Language features

- written in the **past tense** because these are specific events that only happened once
- focus on **specific people, places, dates**, etc.
- may be written in the **first** or **third person**
- **words and devices** to show **time order**

This usually means proper nouns, so remember the capital letters!

Stick to one or the other – don't mix them up

First ..., next ..., finally ..., In 1950 ..., Some weeks later ...

Basic skeleton for making notes is a timeline

An example of a recount text

Toby's Diary

After lunch I washed up for Mum. There wasn't much to wash so we didn't use the dishwasher. I had to fill the washing-up bowl twice, once to wash and once to rinse. I measured seven one-litre jugfuls of water in the bowl each time.

Afterwards, Mum set the washing machine going. Mum said that nearly half the clothes in that load were mine, so I was responsible for half the water the washing machine used!

I went to the toilet twice during the afternoon and washed my hands afterwards. To wash my hands I used the litre jug to put water in the handbasin. I used two half-jugfuls both times.

When Dad got back from his work at the shop, we washed the car. It took seven buckets of water. I didn't use the hosepipe because it would have been too difficult to measure how much water we used.

When we went inside I had some juice mixed with 200 ml of tap water. Next I had a very quick shower before tea. I was only under the shower for about one minute because I was in a rush but keeping the water diary made me realize how often I spend quite a while in there!

At five o'clock I helped make my own tea because I wanted to see how much water would be used. First I washed some potatoes in about one litre of water. Then Mum made some chips with them while I poured nearly a litre of water in a saucepan to warm up frankfurters. I drank a glass of fizzy water (300 millilitres) with my meal. Dad used the dishwasher to wash up afterwards.

Apart from a glass of milk at bedtime, I didn't drink anything else. I went to the toilet and washed my hands and face (1 litre). I forgot to be careful with water and left the tap running when I brushed my teeth. In bed I wrote this diary entry, using the notes I had been keeping all day.

Language features and style of the recount text

Toby's Diary

Past tense throughout, e.g. *washed*

After lunch I washed up for Mum. There wasn't much to wash so we didn't use the dishwasher. I had to fill the washing-up bowl twice, once to wash and once to rinse. I measured seven one-litre jugfuls of water in the bowl each time.

Written in the first person

Connectives that signal time

Afterwards, Mum set the washing machine going. Mum said that nearly half the clothes in that load were mine, so I was responsible for half the water the washing machine used!

Specific people referred to, e.g. I, we, Mum, Dad

I went to the toilet twice during the afternoon and washed my hands afterwards. To wash my hands I used the litre jug to put water in the handbasin. I used two half-jugfuls both times.

Detail included to interest the reader

When Dad got back from his work at the shop, we washed the car. It took seven buckets of water. I didn't use the hosepipe because it would have been too difficult to measure how much water we used.

Writing organized in paragraphs, each paragraph outlining a particular aspect of the recount

When we went inside I had some juice mixed with 200ml of tap water. Next I had a very quick shower before tea. I was only under the shower for about one minute because I was in a rush but keeping the water diary made me realize how often I spend quite a while in there!

Informal style

At five o'clock I helped make my own tea because I wanted to see how much water would be used. First I washed some potatoes in about one litre of water. Then Mum made some chips with them while I poured nearly a litre of water in a saucepan to warm up frankfurters. I drank a glass of fizzy water (300 millilitres) with my meal. Dad used the dishwasher to wash up afterwards.

Past tense verbs

Connectives that signal time

Apart from a glass of milk at bedtime, I didn't drink anything else. I went to the toilet and washed my hands and face (1 litre). I forgot to be careful with water and left the tap running when I brushed my teeth. In bed I wrote this diary entry, using the notes I had been keeping all day.

Closing statement commenting on events

Content and organization of the recount text

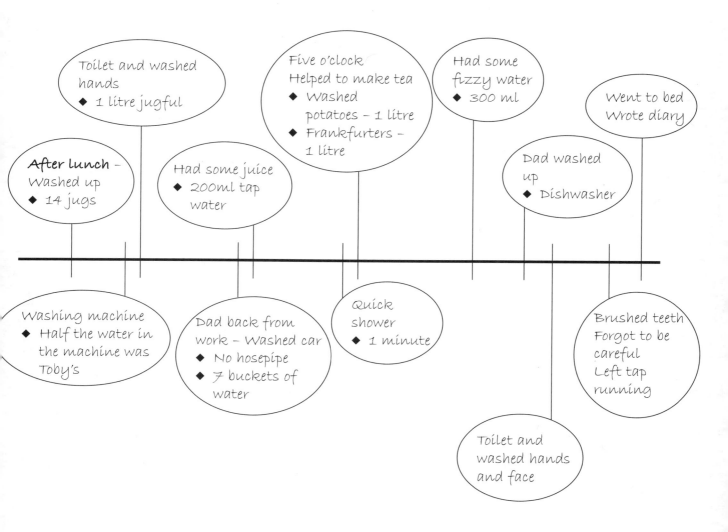

Toilet and washed hands
- ◆ 1 litre jugful

After lunch –
Washed up
- ◆ 14 jugs

Had some juice
- ◆ 200ml tap water

Five o'clock
Helped to make tea
- ◆ Washed potatoes – 1 litre
- ◆ Frankfurters – 1 litre

Had some fizzy water
- ◆ 300 ml

Dad washed up
- ◆ Dishwasher

Went to bed
Wrote diary

Washing machine
- ◆ Half the water in the machine was Toby's

Dad back from work – Washed car
- ◆ No hosepipe
- ◆ 7 buckets of water

Quick shower
- ◆ 1 minute

Toilet and washed hands and face

Brushed teeth
Forgot to be careful
Left tap running

Teaching pupils how to read and write instruction text

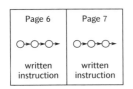

Page 6	Page 7
written instruction	written instruction

Reading an instruction text

Read pp 6–7 of *Water and Rivers* pupils' book with the pupils. You will need:

- The written instructions on pp 6–7 (the text-only version on p 27 of these notes can be enlarged/photocopied/made into an OHT for annotation)
- p 26 of these notes enlarged/photocopied/made into OHTs for annotation

SHARED READING ACTIVITY

Audience and purpose

Talk about how the intended audience and purpose affects language and layout.

Audience – other pupils/anyone who wants to know how to make a rain gauge.
Purpose – to describe how something is done through a series of sequenced steps.

SHARED WRITING ACTIVITY

Content and organization

Show pupils how the content of this instruction text is organized by demonstrating its contents in an instruction skeleton (see example on p 29 of these notes). Each stage in the process is represented in note form in a box on the instruction skeleton. Boxes may also be included to show the materials needed.

SHARED READING ACTIVITY

Language features and style

Return to the text and discuss the way language has been used to support the reader when attempting to follow the instructions, e.g. written in the imperative tense; *discard* the lids, *cut* the top, *fill* the jug. Also stress the importance of the stages in the process being written in chronological order and the use of numbered bullet points to signpost to the reader which step comes next (see annotated example on p 28 of these notes).

INDEPENDENT ACTIVITY

Independent activity

Working in groups of three the pupils make a rain gauge. One of the members of the group reads out the instructions following the skeleton. The other two members, however, have no access to the instructions (either from the page or the skeleton) and have to follow the oral instructions. Evaluate the instructions and discuss whether there was anything that they had to add to them, e.g. if there were any steps missing.

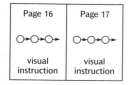
Writing an instruction text

Use pp 16–17 of *Water and Rivers* pupils' book as a basis for pupils' own instruction texts. You will need:

◆ the visual instruction on pp 16–17
◆ p 26 of these notes enlarged/ photocopied/ made into OHTs for annotation

> SHARED
> READING
> ACTIVITY

Content and organization

Revise the content and organization of the instruction text from the previous session (see p 29 of these notes).

> PAIRED
> READING AND
> WRITING
> ACTIVITY

Pairs of pupils discuss the visual instructions on pp 16–17 of the pupils' book and make instruction skeleton notes (see below). Notes should include content of the pages, details from the pictures, labels and any further information they may know.

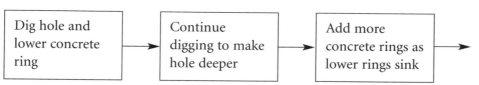

Language features and style

Remind pupils of the language features and style of instructions (see p 26 of these notes).

Audience and purpose

Discuss the audience for pupils' instructions (other pupils/readers who want to know how to build a well) and the purpose (to give step-by-step instructions on how to build a well).

> SHARED
> WRITING
> ACTIVITY

Demonstrate how to write the first bullet point, for example:

1. First dig a shallow hole. The hole should be approx. 1 m deep.

Draw attention to the fact that you are using the imperative form of the verb and that you are using generalized agents rather than named individuals.

Ask pupils to make suggestions for the next instruction, ensuring that they use clear and concise sentences to prevent the reader from becoming muddled.

2. Lower the first concrete ring into the hole.

Discuss the use of temporal connectives as additional signposts as to the order of the instructions, e.g. *next, after that, then. . . .*

> INDEPENDENT
> WRITING
> ACTIVITY

Independent activity

Pupils to complete the instructions ensuring they include the key features discussed.

About instruction text

Audience and purpose

Audience – someone who needs to use the instructions

Purpose – to tell someone how to do or make something

> Sometimes you may know more about the age or interests of your reader

Content and organization

- **title** (or opening sentence) tells what is to be done or made

> How to make a . . .

- **list** of what is needed

> You will need: 2 sheets of A4 white paper, coloured pens . . . etc

- sometimes **picture(s) or diagram(s)**
- the instructions are written as a sequence in **time order**

> 1. Draw a person . . .
> 2. Cut it out . . .

Language features

- written in the **imperative,** as if the writer is talking directly to the reader telling him or her what to do

> Draw a person . . . Cut it out . . .

- numbers or words and devices to show the **sequence** of the steps

> First . . . next . . . Finally . . .

- all **necessary detail** included (for instance, *how many, how far, how long*)
- **factual descriptive words,** not like the descriptions in a story

> 2 A4 sheets of white paper

> NOT two lovely sheets of clean, crisp, white paper!

Basic skeleton for making notes is a flowchart

An example of an instruction text

How to make a rain gauge

A rain gauge is used to measure rainfall in a particular area to reproduce rainfall graphs like those on page 9.

You will need:
sharp scissors
waterproof pen
ruler
measuring jug with cc (cubic centimetre) scale
1.5 litre clear plastic soft drinks bottle
300–500 ml, clear, straight sided plastic bottle (e.g. empty bubble bath bottle)

1. Discard the lids from both the bottles, then wash the bottles thoroughly.

2. Cut the top off the soft drinks bottle about 8 cm down from the neck of the bottle. Cut a straight edge all around.

3. Cut the top off the smaller plastic bottle. The cut should be below the bottle's neck.

4. Fill the measuring jug with 100 cc of water. Check the measure is accurate.

5. Pour the water into the smaller plastic bottle. Mark the water level on the side of the bottle with the waterproof pen.

6. Fill the bottle with another 100 cc measure and mark the next water level. Repeat several times to create a scale up the side of the bottle. Use the ruler to make sure the scale goes straight up one side of the bottle.

7. Pour the water out of the bottle. Next place it upright in the bottom section of the soft drinks bottle.

8. Use the top of the drinks bottle and place upside down in the top of the smaller bottle to act as a funnel.

9. Place the rain gauge upright in a hole in the ground outside, so that the top of the funnel is 300 mm above ground level.

10. Check the water level in the bottle and record the readings every morning.

Language features and style of the instruction text

◆ Present tense throughout
◆ Imperative form of the verb
◆ Generic participant rather than named individual
◆ Formal factual style
◆ Chronological
◆ Short clear sentences

How to make a rain gauge

A rain gauge is used to measure rainfall in a particular area to reproduce rainfall graphs like those on page 9.

You will need:
sharp scissors
waterproof pen
ruler
measuring jug with cc (cubic centimetre) scale
1.5 litre clear plastic soft drinks bottle
300–500 ml, clear, straight sided plastic bottle (e.g. empty bubble bath bottle)

1. Discard the lids from both the bottles, then wash the bottles thoroughly.

2. Cut the top off the soft drinks bottle about 8 cm down from the neck of the bottle. Cut a straight edge all around.

3. Cut the top off the smaller plastic bottle. The cut should be below the bottle's neck.

4. Fill the measuring jug with 100 cc of water. Check the measure is accurate.

5. Pour the water into the smaller plastic bottle. Mark the water level on the side of the bottle with the waterproof pen.

6. Fill the bottle with another 100 cc measure and mark the next water level. Repeat several times to create a scale up the side of the bottle. Use the ruler to make sure the scale goes straight up one side of the bottle.

7. Pour the water out of the bottle. Next place it upright in the bottom section of the soft drinks bottle.

8. Use the top of the drinks bottle and place upside down in the top of the smaller bottle to act as a funnel.

9. Place the rain gauge upright in a hole in the ground outside, so that the top of the funnel is 300 mm above ground level.

10. Check the water level in the bottle and record the readings every morning.

Annotations

- Title indicates what you are writing about
- Opening statement sets out what is to be achieved
- List of items required
- Imperative form of the verb
- Numbered bullet points signalling order of steps in sequence
- Connectives signalling time
- Sequence of steps outlining process. Written in chronological order
- Second statement enlarging on first and ensuring precision
- Adjectives and adverbs used only when necessary

Content and organization of the instruction text

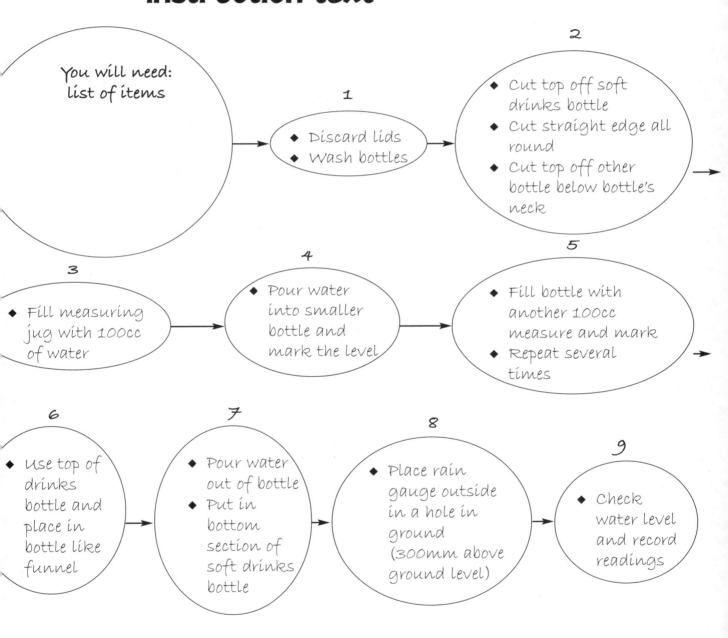

You will need: list of items

1
◆ Discard lids
◆ Wash bottles

2
◆ Cut top off soft drinks bottle
◆ Cut straight edge all round
◆ Cut top off other bottle below bottle's neck

3
◆ Fill measuring jug with 100cc of water

4
◆ Pour water into smaller bottle and mark the level

5
◆ Fill bottle with another 100cc measure and mark
◆ Repeat several times

6
◆ Use top of drinks bottle and place in bottle like funnel

7
◆ Pour water out of bottle
◆ Put in bottom section of soft drinks bottle

8
◆ Place rain gauge outside in a hole in ground (300mm above ground level)

9
◆ Check water level and record readings

Teaching pupils how to read and write report text

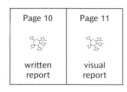

Page 10	Page 11
written report	visual report

Reading a report text

Read p 10 of *Water and Rivers* pupils' book with the pupils. You will need:

◆ the written report on p 10 (the text-only version on p 33 of these notes can be enlarged/photocopied/made into an OHT for annotation)

◆ p 32 of these notes enlarged/photocopied/made into OHTs for annotation

> **SHARED READING ACTIVITY**

Audience and purpose

Talk about how the intended audience and purpose affects language and layout.

Audience – school pupils, who may know little about the subject.

Purpose – to provide factual information about droughts and floods.

> **SHARED WRITING ACTIVITY**

Content and organization

Show pupils how the content of this report text is organized by demonstrating its content in a report skeleton (see p 35 of these notes). Each paragraph becomes one arm of the report skeleton and details are noted around it.

> **SHARED READING ACTIVITY**

Language features and style

Return to the text and talk about the way language has been used to achieve the effects the author intended (see annotated version on p 34 of these notes). Note useful features for later use in pupils' own writing, e.g. clear presentation of factual information.

> **INDEPENDENT ACTIVITY**

Independent activity

Pupils use the report skeleton to form a television news style report. Use a drama session to deliver the report in the style of a newscaster to the rest of the class. A freeze-frame activity could be done to illustrate the report (other pupils act out the people in the drought areas).

Writing a report text

Use p 11 of *Water and Rivers* pupils' book as a basis for pupils's own report texts. You will need:

◆ the visual report on p 11
◆ p 32 of these notes enlarged/ photocopied/made into OHTs for annotation

SHARED READING ACTIVITY

Content and organization

Revise the content and organization of the report text from the previous session (see p 35 of these notes).

PAIRED READING AND WRITING ACTIVITY

Pairs of pupils read the visual report on p 11 of the pupils' book and begin to discuss how sections of the report skeleton notes may be formed into paragraphs (pupils may want to make additional notes). Consider the order of the paragraphs and if any additional information needs to be included, e.g. details from the pictures.

Language features and style

Remind pupils of the language features and style of reports (see p 34 of these notes).

Audience and purpose

Discuss the audience for pupils' reports (readers who know nothing about flooding in India) and the purpose (to give basic factual information about the situation).

SHARED WRITING ACTIVITY

Explain to pupils that they will be writing in the style of a newspaper report (use examples from shared reading to illustrate this). Discuss the use of facts and evidence to elaborate on points being made in each paragraph.

Demonstrate writing a short introductory paragraph, for example:

Excess rainfall caused destruction and devastation for people living in eastern India. In September 2000, annual monsoon rains were heavier than usual and created mass flooding which destroyed the local community.

Ask pupils to work in pairs to create the next paragraph about the flood victims, using information outlined in the report skeleton. For example:

208 people died as a result of the flooding and another 165 people have been reported missing. In isolated villages families found themselves clambering onto rooftops in an attempt to avoid the rising waters.

INDEPENDENT WRITING ACTIVITY

Pupils continue and complete the report independently.

About report text

Audience and purpose

Audience – someone who wants to know about the topic

Purpose – to describe what something is like

> Sometimes you may know more about the age or interests of your reader

Content and organization

- **non-chronological** information
- **introductory sentence or paragraph** says what the report is going to be about
- the information is sorted into groups or **categories**
- reports may include short pieces of explanation

> This means it ISN'T written in time order, like a story or recount

> what something looks like, where it is found ...

Language features

- written in the **present tense**
- usually **general nouns and pronouns** (not particular people or things)
- **factual descriptive words**, not like the descriptions in a story
- words and devices that show **comparison and contrast**
- **third person** writing to make the report **impersonal and formal**
- **technical words and phrases** –which you may need to explain to the reader
- use of **examples** to help the reader understand the technical words

> you would write about dogs in general, not a particular dog

> You would say *powerful beams*, not *beautiful bright beams*

> Expressions like *have in common, the same as ..., on the other hand, however...*

> unusual words that go with the topic such as, *canine, translucent* and *wing span*

> *wingspan* is the length of a bird's wing

Basic skeleton for making notes is a spidergram

An example of a report text

3 years of drought in Africa

People in south-eastern Ethiopia are suffering from a third consecutive year of drought. An estimated 13 million people are affected. In the Ogaden District alone, 1.2 million people face the danger of starvation.

South-eastern Ethiopia has been described as a dust bowl. The lack of rain has turned the region into a hot, dry and inhospitable area. Plants cannot survive, so very few crops are being harvested. Grasses are drying up, leaving animals without pastureland.

Around 70 per cent of the people in the region are nomadic, which means they travel around looking for fresh water and pasture for their livestock. However in this drought-stricken area, both are almost non-existent, and so many animals have died. If any have survived, farmers have been forced to sell them to buy food.

Thousands of people have left the region to escape the dust and heat, and in search of aid. People who have nothing are waiting for help from local and national aid agencies. In one village, 3000 people have settled in a temporary refugee camp. They have nothing but their makeshift homes built from cardboard or animal skins.

At one camp, one in ten pupils have died because of the lack of medicines to treat their hunger-related diseases. In some areas, food-aid stations have not yet been set up. Even in places where there are aid stations, supplies are running out.

Aid agencies have been begging for help for months. Since television has brought images of suffering into people's homes, there have been many promises of help. However, it takes time to get supplies where they are needed. Civil war in the region makes it difficult for aid agencies to operate safely. Bandits ambush trucks carrying supplies. One agency worker said, "It is a difficult task, but we have to get the aid to where it is needed quickly. For many, it is already too late."

Language features and style of the report text

- Present tense throughout, e.g. *are*
- General nouns throughout, e.g. *people*
- Style formal, factual
- Third person
- Non-chronological

3 years of drought in Africa

Introductory paragraph outlining what the text will be about

Factual evidence to back up main points

People in south-eastern Ethiopia are suffering from a third consecutive year of drought. An estimated 13 million people are affected. In the Ogaden District alone, 1.2 million people face the danger of starvation.

Technical term defined in following sentence

Information about region

South-eastern Ethiopia has been described as a dust bowl. The lack of rain has turned the region into a hot, dry and inhospitable area. Plants cannot survive, so very few crops are being harvested. Grasses are drying up, leaving animals without pastureland.

factual adjectives

Information about inhabitants

Around 70 per cent of the people in the region are nomadic, which means they travel around looking for fresh water and pasture for their livestock. However in this drought-stricken area, both are almost non-existent, and so many animals have died. If any have survived, farmers have been forced to sell them to buy food.

factual adjectives

Information about refugees

Thousands of people have left the region to escape the dust and heat, and in search of aid. People who have nothing are waiting for help from local and national aid agencies. In one village, 3000 people have settled in a temporary refugee camp. They have nothing but their makeshift homes built from cardboard or animal skins.

General nouns

Information about camps

At one camp, one in ten children have died because of the lack of medicines to treat their hunger related diseases. In some areas, food aid stations have not yet been set up. Even in places where there are aid stations, supplies are running out.

Use of example to add more information

Information about aid agencies

Factual adverb

Aid agencies have been begging for help for months. Since television has brought images of suffering into people's homes, there have been many promises of help. However, it takes time to get supplies where they are needed. Civil war in the region makes it difficult for aid agencies to operate safely. Bandits ambush trucks carrying supplies. One agency worker said, 'It is a difficult task, but we have to get the aid to where it is needed quickly. For many, it is already too late.'

Contrasting statement as a sentence opening

Content and organization of the report text

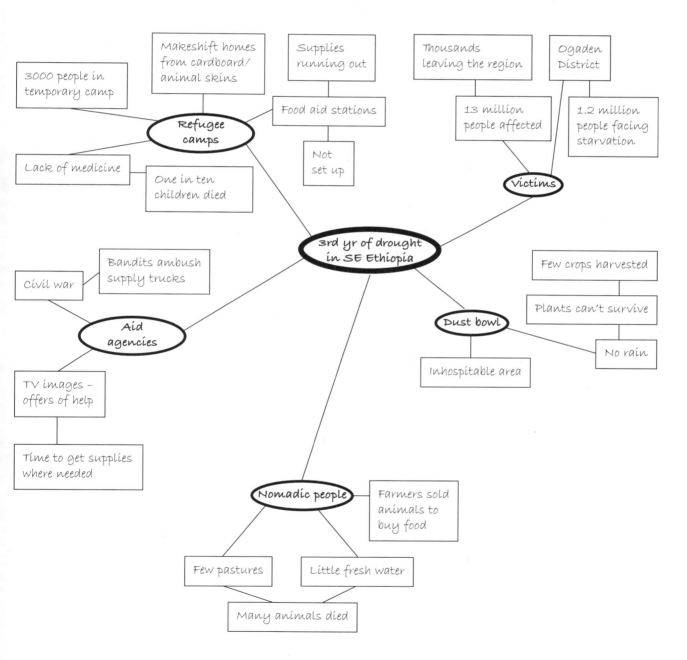

Teaching pupils how to read and write explanation text

Page 22	Page 23
⟲⇄⟲	⟲⇄⟲
written explanation	written explanation

Reading an explanation text

Read pp 22–23 of *Water and Rivers* pupils' book with the pupils. You will need:

◆ the written explanation on pp 22–23 (the text-only version on p 39 of these notes can be enlarged/ photocopied/ made into an OHT for annotation)

◆ p 38 of these notes enlarged/ photocopied/ made into an OHT for annotation

> SHARED READING ACTIVITY

Audience and purpose

Talk about how the intended audience and purpose affects language and layout.

Audience – general audience who may know little about the subject.
Purpose – to explain how something works.

> SHARED WRITING ACTIVITY

Content and organization

Show pupils how the context of this explanation is organized by demonstrating its content in an explanation skeleton (see p 41 of these notes).

> SHARED READING ACTIVITY

Language features and style

Return to the text and talk about the way language has been used to achieve the effects the author intended (see annotated version on p 40 in these notes). Draw attention to the use of technical vocabulary, e.g. *valves, plumbing, mains water supply etc*. Discuss how it is sometimes effective to use diagrams to support the information in the written text.

> INDEPENDENT ACTIVITY

Independent activity

Using the explanation skeleton notes, create a list of questions to ask the caretaker.

Make large cards with the various stages of 'Moving water' taken from the skeleton – ask some pupils to hold them and to line up (not in the correct order). Ask the rest of the class if they can put the cards in order.

Writing an explanation text

Use pp 36–37 of *Water and Rivers* pupils' book as a basis for pupils' own explanation texts. You will need:

- the visual explanation on pp 36–37
- p 38 of these notes enlarged/photocopied/made into OHTs for annotation

SHARED
READING
ACTIVITY

Content and organization

Revise the content and organization of the explanation text from the previous session (see p 41 of these notes).

PAIRED
READING AND
WRITING
ACTIVITY

In pairs, ask pupils to discuss the visual explanation on pp 36–37 of the pupils' book and make explanation skeleton notes (see below). Notes should include details from the pictures and captions in addition to information pupils already know. Discuss the notes and improve if necessary.

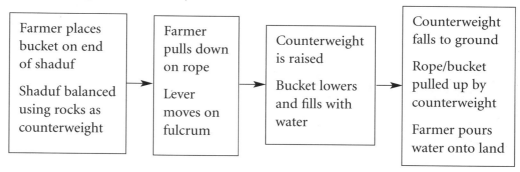

Farmer places bucket on end of shaduf

Shaduf balanced using rocks as counterweight

→

Farmer pulls down on rope

Lever moves on fulcrum

→

Counterweight is raised

Bucket lowers and fills with water

→

Counterweight falls to ground

Rope/bucket pulled up by counterweight

Farmer pours water onto land

Language features and style

Remind pupils of the language feature and style of explanation texts (see p 40 of these notes).

Audience and purpose

Discuss the audience for pupils' explanations (readers who know nothing about a shaduf) and the purpose (to explain clearly how a shaduf works).

SHARED
WRITING
ACTIVITY

Using the opening paragraph provided in the text as an introduction, demonstrate by writing a short paragraph to explore how the shaduf is made, e.g.

The shaduf is created using a long beam with a thin end and a wider end balanced on a support called a fulcrum. The beam is weighted at one end with rocks and a bucket is attached to the thinner end with a rope.

Explain to the pupils that you are going to use the next paragraph to begin to tell the reader how the shaduf works, e.g.

In order to lower the bucket, the farmer pulls on the rope. This causes the beam to move on the fulcrum and the counterweight lifts in the air.

Draw attention to the connectives that have been used and explain that they show cause and effect.

Ask pupils in pairs to use individual whiteboards to write the next two sentences, emphasizing the use of causal connectives and the use of technical vocabulary.

INDEPENDENT
WRITING
ACTIVITY

Independent writing

Pupils write up the next two paragraphs independently.

About explanation text

Audience and purpose

Audience – someone who wants to understand the process (how or why it happens)

Purpose – to explain how or why something happens

Sometimes you may know more about the age or interests of your reader

Content and organization

- **title** often asks a question, or says clearly what the explanation is about
- text often opens with **general statement(s)** to introduce important words or ideas
- the process is then written in a **series of logical steps**, usually in **time order**
- sometimes picture(s) or diagram(s)

This happens...then this happens... next...

Language features

- **third person** writing to make the explanation **impersonal and formal**
- written in the **present tense**
- usually **general nouns and pronouns** (not particular people or things)
- **factual descriptive words**, not like the descriptions in a story
- **technical words and phrases** –which you may need to explain to the reader
- words and devices that show **sequence**
- words and devices that show **cause and effect**

You would say powerful beams, not beautiful bright beams

unusual words that go with the topic such as, canine, translucent and wingspan

you would write about dogs in general, not a particular dog

First..., next..., finally

If..., then... This happens because... This means that...

Basic skeleton for making notes is a flowchart

The explanation skeleton can change depending on the sort of process

An example of an explanation text

Moving water

In a house, there are many water pipes through which water flows. The pipes, tanks and controls, such as valves, allow for the safe passage of water in, around and out of a house. They are part of the entire water system in a building which is known as the plumbing.

Clean, cold water arrives from the mains water supply via a communication pipe. The pipe joins the householder's service pipe at a stopcock (control valve) underground near the boundary of the property. The water company, which supplies water to houses, can use the stopcock to turn the householder's water supply on or off. The householder's service pipe may be fitted with a meter for measuring the amount of water used.

The service pipe goes up into the house where it reaches another stopcock, usually under the kitchen sink. This valve is turned off when plumbing repairs in the house are necessary. The pipe (often called the rising main) then takes water up to the kitchen sink, and may branch off to other fixtures such as a washing machine. In older houses, the rising main also takes water up to a cold-water storage tank, high up in the house. The water passes up vertically – without trickling back – because of the pressure of the water in the mains.

From the tank, the cold water travels down to other water outlets and appliances, such as taps, showers, toilet cisterns and water-heating systems. Water is usually heated in a boiler, stored in a cylinder and then piped to hot-water taps or other appliances.

While the water system of pipes brings clean water into a house, another system takes waste and dirty water away. This drainage system consists of larger pipes that lead to a single 'soil and waste' stack. This wide, vertical pipe drains all the waste water and solids to underground drains.

The drains usually lead to a water company's sewer, which takes the waste to a sewage works for treatment.

Language features and style of an explanation text

Moving water

title demonstrating what the explanation is going to be about

In a house, there are many water pipes through which water flows. The pipes, tanks and controls, such as valves, allow for the safe passage of water in, around and out of a house. They are part of the entire water system in a building which is known as the plumbing.

present tense verb

technical word (explained to the reader in first part of sentence)

Clean, cold water arrives from the **mains water** supply via a communication pipe. The pipe joins the householder's service pipe at a stopcock (control valve) underground near the boundary of the property. The water company, which supplies water to houses, can use the stopcock to turn the householder's water supply on or off. The householder's service pipe may be fitted with a meter for measuring the amount of water used.

general noun rather then specific

use of brackets to provide definitions of technical words

The service pipe goes up into the house where it reaches another stopcock, usually under the kitchen sink. This valve is turned off when plumbing repairs in the house are necessary. The pipe (often called the rising main) then takes water up to the kitchen sink, and may branch off to other fixtures such as a washing machine. In older houses, the rising main also takes water up to a cold-water storage tank, high up in the house. The water passes up vertically – without trickling back – because of the pressure of the water in the mains.

Words and devices to signal time

Words and devices to show cause and effect

From the tank, the cold water travels down to other water outlets and appliances, such as taps, showers, toilet cisterns and water-heating systems. Water is usually heated in a boiler, stored in a cylinder and then piped to hot-water taps or other appliances.

General noun rather than specific

While the water system of pipes brings clean water into a house, another system takes waste and dirty water away. This drainage system consists of larger pipes that lead to a single 'soil and waste' stack. This wide, vertical pipe drains all the waste water and solids to underground drains.

technical phrase

The drains usually lead to a water company's sewer, which takes the waste to a sewage works for treatment.

Content and organization of the explanation text

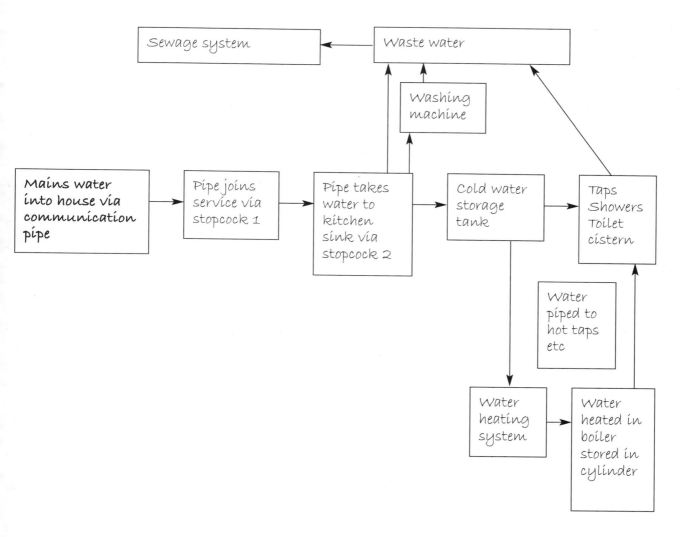

Teaching pupils how to read and write persuasion text

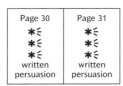

Page 30	Page 31
✳⟨ ✳⟨ ✳⟨	✳⟨ ✳⟨ ✳⟨
written persuasion	written persuasion

Reading a persuasion text

Read pp 30–31 of *Water and Rivers* pupils' book with the pupils. You will need:

◆ the written persuasion on pp 30–31 (the text-only version on p 45 of these notes can be enlarged/photocopied/made into an OHT for annotation)

◆ p 44 of these notes enlarged/photocopied/made into OHTs for annotation

> SHARED READING ACTIVITY

Audience and purpose

When reading the letters, discuss how the tone and style is altered depending on the purpose of the letter and the audience. Focus on the more formal tone of the letter on p 31 of the pupils' book.

Audience – disgruntled water company customer.
Purpose – to convince the reader that the water company is providing an essential service at a reasonable price.

> SHARED WRITING ACTIVITY

Content and organization

Using the letter on p 31 show pupils how the content of this persuasion text is organized, by demonstrating its content in a basic bullet and elaboration skeleton (see example on p 47 of these notes). Each paragraph becomes one bullet point and details are noted next to it.

When reading the text you will also need to draw attention to the fact that the text is written in the form of a letter. Such letters have certain conventions which need to be adhered to, such as the inclusion of the address and date, the form of address and the signing off.

> SHARED READING ACTIVITY

Language features and style

Return to the text and talk about the way language has been used to achieve the effects the author intended (see annotated version on p 46). Note key features of persuasive writing such as, the use of facts/ evidence to back up main points, e.g. *scientific reports tell us. . . .*; the use of strong, positive language e.g. *excellent service, reasonable price.*

> INDEPENDENT ACTIVITY

Independent activity

Pupils make a skeleton of the letter on p 30 of the pupils' book. In pairs, pupils choose which perspective they want to take – the customer or the water company. Then, using the persuasion skeletons as prompts, they have to take turns in asking questions and then answering them from the chosen perspective – hot seat exercise.

Writing a persuasion text

Use pp 18–19 of *Water and Rivers* pupils' book as a basis for pupils' own persuasion texts. You will need:

◆ the visual persusasion on pp 18–19

◆ p 44 of this book enlarged/ photocopied/ made into OHTs for annotation

> SHARED READING ACTIVITY

Content and organization

Revise the content and organization of persuasion text from the previous session (see p 47 of these notes).

> PAIRED READING AND WRITING ACTIVITY

Ask pupils to work in pairs and discuss the visual persuasion on pp 18–19 in the pupils' book. Explore the idea that both sides of the argument are presented and explain to pupils that they are going to choose one aspect of the debate to focus on. Outline the fact that pupils will be writing a letter of complaint to the authorities expressing concerns about the building of the dam. Using the visual persuasion as a basis, ask pupils to make persuasion skeleton notes using the basic bullet and elaboration format (see below):

◆ project as waste of money ⟨ $US 29 billion / will cause more harm than good

Language features and style

Remind pupils of the language features and style of persuasive writing (see p 44 of these notes). Also revisit the key features of formal letter writing (as explored in shared reading session).

Audience and purpose

Discuss the audience for pupils' persuasive letters (authorities involved in the commissioning and building of the dam) and the purpose (to persuade the reader that the dam is not a good idea).

> SHARED WRITING ACTIVITY

Demonstrate the writing of the initial layout and opening paragraph of the letter, for example:

Dear Sir,

I am writing to express my grave concern at your planned project for building the Three Gorges Dam. Not only will the proposed dam cost an immense amount of money, but the cost to the environment will be irreparable.

Demonstrate the use of the skeleton notes to show the organization of the paragraphs contained within the letter. Ask pupils to orally compose the next two sentences basing the information on the environmental costs created by the dam building, e.g.

Your proposed building of this dam will lead to a huge loss of wildlife in the surrounding area. This in turn will damage ecosystems. Surely your company does not wish to be responsible for destroying wildlife by taking away their natural habitats?

> INDEPENDENT WRITING ACTIVITY

Independent writing activity

Pupils complete the letter of complaint using the format outlined and employing some of the key features of persuasion text.

As an extension task, some pupils may be asked to present the opposing argument in the form of a letter of response.

✻ About persuasion text

Audience and purpose

Audience – someone you want to persuade, but who may not know much about the subject.

Purpose – to argue the case for a point of view, persuade someone to buy something or support a cause

> Sometimes you may know more about the age or interests of your reader

Content and organization

- usually starts with a sentence or paragraph to **introduce the argument**
- the argument is then split into a number of **main points,** each of which probably needs some **elaboration**
- **concluding sentence or paragraph** sums up the argument

> You may have to introduce some important words or ideas the reader needs to know

> The elaboration could be
> – reasons for agreeing with the point
> – examples to back it up
> – further information to explain it.

Language features

- writing may be personal (**first and second person**) or impersonal (**third person**)
- written in the **present tense**
- language may be quite **emotional**, more like a story than other non-fiction
- there may be **rhetorical questions,** which do not really expect an answer
- words and devices showing **cause and effect,** used to **argue** the case
- words and devices that show movement from one point to the next

> Use powerful verbs and adjectives, exaggerations or repetition to make an effect

> Is this really important?

> Firstly . . ., Another reason that . . ., Thirdly . . .

> Therefore . . ., Consequently . . ., This means that . . .

Basic skeleton for making notes is pronged bullet points

An example of persuasion text

Trimline water company

Mr Jake Spencer
14 Totts Road
Coltersbridge
Westshire
WS9 7TR

5 April 2002

Dear Mr Spencer

I was sorry to receive your letter of complaint, as we are committed to providing our customers with an excellent service at a reasonable price.

Yes, water is a natural resource, but rainwater cannot be used in the home without being treated first. You can safely water your garden with it, but you cannot drink it and you cannot cook with it. If you did you would be seriously endangering your health.

Trimline does not pretend to own rain. However, charges are made for the treatment and purification of water. Trimline constructs, maintains and operates treatment centres, purification processes, storage facilities and pipeline networks. Without these you would not have a constant, reliable, supply of clean, safe water.

I am sure you haven't forgotten that part of your water bill also covers the cost of removing and treating you waste water and sewage. You could treat these in your own home or garden of course, but you would require expensive equipment and a septic tank.

Water may fill the local lake today, but it could run dry tomorrow. Scientific reports tell us that without doubt temperatures in the UK will go up, possibly leading to terrible droughts in the future. Trimline is spending more money on water storage so that if there is a summer of searing heat, cool water will still run from your tap.

I am sorry that we cannot revise your bill, but I am sure in the light of above you will see that we are fulfilling our commitment towards providing water and sewage treatment services at a reasonable price.

Yours sincerely

Margaret Headley
Manager

Language features and style of a persuasion text

Trimline water company

Mr Jake Spencer
14 Totts Road
Coltersbridge
Westshire
WS9 7TR

5 April 2002

Dear Mr Spencer

| Introductory sentence |

I was sorry to receive your letter of complaint, as we are committed to providing our customers with an excellent service at a reasonable price.

| Emotive language |

| Answering a question – speaking directly to reader |

Yes, water is a natural resource, but rainwater cannot be used in the home without being treated first. You can safely water your garden with it, but you cannot drink it and you cannot cook with it. If you did you would be seriously endangering your health.

| Language to persuade reader personally |

| Present tense |

Trimline does not pretend to own rain. However, charges are made for the treatment and purification of water. Trimline constructs, maintains and operates treatment centres, purification processes, storage facilities and pipeline networks. Without these you would not have a constant, reliable, supply of clean, safe water.

| Rhetorical question |

I am sure you haven't forgotten that part of your water bill also covers the cost of removing and treating you waste water and sewage. You could treat these in your own home garden of course, but you would require expensive equipment and a septic tank.

| Factual evidence to back up arguments |

Water may fill the local lake today, but it could run dry tomorrow. Scientific reports tell us that without doubt temperatures in the UK will go up, possibly leading to terrible droughts in the future. Trimline is spending more money on water storage so that if there is a summer of searing heat, cool water will still run from your tap.

| Language to get reader on side |

| Repetition of apology |

I am sorry that we cannot revise your bill, but I am sure in the light of above you will see that we are fulfilling our commitment towards providing water and sewage treatment services at a reasonable price.

| Repeating words for effect |

| Concluding sentence |

Yours sincerely

Margaret Headley
Manager

If you are using this text with other year groups then highlight the features relevant to that year group, and also these:

Y4/P5 ◆ Words and devices to show cause and effect, words and devices that show movement from one point to another

Content and organization of persuasion text

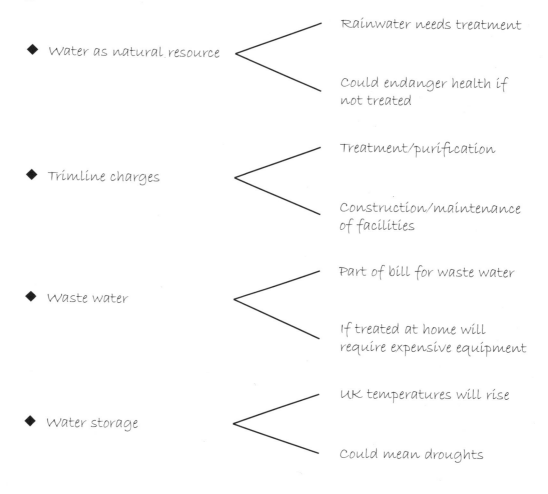

◆ Water as natural resource
- Rainwater needs treatment
- Could endanger health if not treated

◆ Trimline charges
- Treatment/purification
- Construction/maintenance of facilities

◆ Waste water
- Part of bill for waste water
- If treated at home will require expensive equipment

◆ Water storage
- UK temperatures will rise
- Could mean droughts

Page	Contents	Text Type	National Literacy Strategy Objectives	QCA Geography Objectives Unit 11 Water Unit 14 Investigating Rivers Pupils should learn:
2	Concept map Contents		T2 TL 17	
4	The Water Cycle	Visual Explanation	T2 TL 15, 21, 22 T2 SL 8, 9 T2 WL 2, 3, 9	• about the water cycle, including condensation and evaporation
6	How to make a rain gauge	Written Instruction	T1 TL 22, 23, 26, 27 T1 SL 8, 9	• about how site conditions can influence the weather
8	Where is the world's water?	Written + visual Report	T2 TL 19, 20, 22, 23, 24 T2 SL 3, 5, 8, 9 T2 WL 2, 3, 9	• to obtain information from maps and an atlas • about world weather patterns • about physical and human features
10	Too little or too much water	Written + Visual Report	T2 TL 20, 22 T2 SL 3, 5, 8, 9 T2 WL 2, 3, 9	
12	Water Diary 1	Visual Recount	T1 TL 21, 23, 24, 26, 27 T1 SL 1, 3, 5 T1 WL 2, 3	• how water is used in the world
14	Helping thirsty people	Written Persuasion	T3 TL 13, 14, 15, 16 T3 SL 4, 7	• about jobs in a settlement • about the environmental impact of a local activity
16	How to build a well	Visual Instruction	T1 TL 22, 23, 25, 26, 27 T1 SL 3, 6, 9 T1 WL 2, 3	
18	Is it a good idea?	Visual Persuasion (Discussion)	T3 TL 13, 14, 15, 16, 18, 19 T3 SL 2, 4, 7 T3 WL 2, 3	
20	Who uses water?	Visual Report	T2 TL 20, 22 T2 SL 3, 5 T2 WL 2, 3, 9	• how water is used in the world • to investigate similarities and differences • about land use patterns
22	Moving water	Written Explanation	T2 TL 15, 19, 20 T2 WL 9	• to use secondary sources • to investigate water supply at local and world scales
24	How is water recycled?	Visual Explanation	T2 TL 15, 19, 20, 22 T2 SL 8, 9 T2 WL 9	• to analyse evidence • use secondary sources • about a land use issue
26	Water diary 2	Written Recount	T1 TL 21, 23, 26, 27 T1 SL 4, 6	• how water is used in the world • to investigate similarities and differences • about land use patterns
28	Save our water!	Written + Visual Persuasion	T3 TL 13, 14, 15, 16, 18, 19 T3 SL 2, 4, 7 T3 WL 2, 3	
30	Who owns water? – I do!	Written Persuasion (Discussion)	T3 TL 12, 14, 15, 16, 17, 19 T3 SL 4, 6, 7	• about jobs in a settlement
32	Why was water a problem in Victorian towns and cities?	Visual Report	T2 TL 18, 20, 22 T2 SL 3, 5, 9, 10 T2 WL 2, 3, 9	• to analyse evidence • use secondary sources
34	Why do people live by the River Nile?	Written Report	T2 TL 20, 22 T2 SL 5, 9	• to investigate places • to use geographical vocabulary • to use atlases and globes • to use secondary sources • about links with other places • about environmental impact
36	How does a shaduf work?	Visual Explanation	T2 TL 15, 22 T2 SL 8, 9 T2 WL 2, 3, 9	• to use secondary sources • to investigate water supply at local and world scales
38	How a river shapes the land	Visual Explanation	T2 TL 15, 22 T2 WL 9	• to use geographical vocabulary • to use secondary sources • about river systems • about environmental impact
40	River Research	Written Recount	T1 TL 21, 23, 26, 27 T1 SL 4, 6	• how rivers erode, transport and deposit materials producing particular landscape features • to use secondary sources of evidence
42	River investigation	Written Instruction	T1 TL 22, 23, 25, 26 T1 SL 3, 9	
44	Glossary		T2 TL 17	
45	Bibliography		T2 TL 17, 18	
47	Index		T2 TL 17	